THE SPLENDOR OF JADE

THE SPLENDOR

Four Thousand Years of the Art of Chinese Jade Carving

OF JADE

by J.J. Schedel

with an Introduction by Professor Na Chih-liang

A Dutton Visual Book ◈

E. P. Dutton & Co., Inc. / New York / 1974

Edited and designed by Nicolas Ducrot

Copyright 1974 in all countries of the International Copyright Union by Joseph J. Schedel. All rights reserved.
First Edition
First published, 1974, in the United States by E. P. Dutton & Co., Inc., 201 Park Avenue South, New York, New York 10003

Published simultaneously in Canada by Clarke, Irwin & Company Limited, Toronto and Vancouver
ISBN: 0-525-49505-3

Library of Congress Cataloging in Publication Data

Schedel, J. J.
The spendor of jade.
(A Dutton visual book)

Bibliography: p.
1. Jade art objects—China—Catalogs.   2. Schedel, J.J.—Art collections.   I. Title.
NK5750.S39   736'.24'0951   74-9855

Printed and bound in Switzerland

Throughout the ages the greatest gift the gods can bestow upon a man is the love of a good woman. I have been extremely fortunate to receive this gift. Therefore, I dedicate this book to Marie Pauline, my loving wife of many years.

The artifacts shown are personally owned and, to my knowledge, have never been publicly described or exhibited. A plate number precedes the description produced by my study of each carving, together with information acquired with the following persons:

Professor Na Chih-liang, Curator of Jade,
National Palace Museum, Taiwan,
Republic of China

Mr. Allain Ramsey, former teacher of Oriental Art,
Buffalo, New York

Text consultants:
Dr. James G. Southworth, Professor Emeritus,
University of Toledo, Toledo, Ohio

and

Mrs. Jane Williams, Toledo, Ohio

Photography by Walbridge & Bellg, Toledo, Ohio
Photographer: John Wehmeyer

CONTENTS

PREFACE

Since the dawn of history men have had dreams of better things. Artisans have translated some of these dreams into ornaments, icons, paintings, and sculptures. These artifacts have been collected by farseeing elders and have been passed from generations to our time. In fact, the temporary ownership has been only a custodianship for those who follow. Jade has been used to express the artist's emotion since the archaic time of the ancient Chinese dynasties. From the first crude effort of the legendary Hsia Dynasty, they evolved their unsurpassed artistry of the Ming and Ch'ing dynasties.

I have attempted to preserve some of these masterpieces for posterity. It is difficult to reproduce, by photographic process, the exquisite hues and the masterful execution of the artist. This book is an intention to share my stewardship with the general public.

J. J. Schedel

INTRODUCTION TO JADE

by
Professor Na Chih-liang
Curator of Jade
National Palace Museum
Taiwan/Republic of China

The art of Chinese jade carving represents a distinct tradition in which the most impressive artistic expressions and excellent craftsmanship, especially in reference to complicated decor of extreme elegance and delicacy, are brought into being through most economical means. It is an art that is not only appreciated and treasured by the Chinese people but is also important in the artistic development of all mankind.

There are three principal aspects of the Chinese jade objects which attract and deserve our immediate attention:

1. The value of jade itself. Jade possesses some of the most

admirable qualities. It is lustrous, subtle, with clear, delightful colors. When one sees a piece of jade, he is immediately compelled to touch it and caress it. Such allure is rarely encountered among other art materials. Indeed, all other artifacts require tremendous modification by human effort before they become aesthetically pleasing; only jade, unique in its natural being, already contains the beautiful qualities that are attractive to man. Whether it is jade, the raw material, or jade, the finished *objet d'art*, it is equally precious and enticing.

In addition to the physical attractiveness of jade, the Chinese perceived its beauty as similar to the beautiful virtues—unpretentiously pure and dignified—of a gentleman or gentlewoman. Therefore, to appreciate and respond to the beauty of jade, one must approach it with a sense of human respect.

Jade has become the natural material not only for decorative ornaments but also for personal adornments. As a literary source, *Yü T'zao*, [Account of] Jade Dressing Ornaments from the *Book of Rites (Li Chi)* (ca. second century A.D.) states that in more ancient times it was customary for a gentleman to be adorned with jade pendants and jade decorative ornaments, and, indeed, his virtues as a gentleman were measured by his jade pendants. This explains the large quantity of jade pendants that have survived from ancient China.

Indeed, the natural beauty of jade easily gained popularity as an artistic material; besides pendants, jade has also been used for imperial emblems, emblems signifying official rank, ceremonial objects, personal gifts and adornments, funerary objects, personal or official seals, and musical instruments.

2. The importance of jade objects in the study of Chinese ethnology and archaeology. In the primitive civilizations of China, utilitarian and decorative objects, though simply made, were highly regarded and preserved with care. For example, stone axes could be used for hunting, farming, and as weapons. In the course of time, metal axes gradually replaced stone ones. Yet people did not relinquish their sentimental attachment completely to the one-time close companion of their everyday life. Therefore, stone axes survived as symbolic emblems and ceremonial objects.

In the Chou era (ca. 1122–221 B.C.) the clever rulers were inspired by these revered old stone tools and used them as a source of artistic inspiration. They were reproduced in jade and used as official symbols of rank; thus the "Kuei" emblem was born. Following the basic format of the stone ax, variations in length of the "Kuei" emblem denoted differences in rank— the higher the status, the longer the "Kuei." However, despite some stylization and modification, the original form of the stone ax survives. Since the stone ax is simple in construction and common in households, it is inevitable that at times the jade "Kuei" emblem could be mistaken for stone, and vice versa, if one was not aware of the social, cultural, and artistic background.

Similarly, the custom of wearing jade beads and Hsi pendants is a tradition that grew out of the wearing of animal bones (Fig. 1) and animal tusks (Fig. 2) in early times.

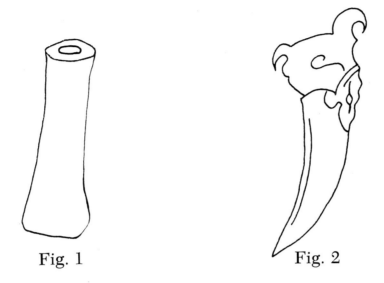

Fig. 1   Fig. 2

Therefore, in order to understand fully the subtle evolution in the development of each and all jade objects in China, one must depend on information provided by ethnological and archaeological studies. Reciprocally, jade objects themselves are also indispensable to these areas of studies.

3. The artistic value of the jade objects. The excellence of jade craftsmanship in China is world-renowned, whether it is simple or extremely delicate and complex. However, the lapidary process and the working method have always remained

essentially the same. They are based on the principle and technique of "stone attacking stone." In other words, to work on jade one uses a similar stone material, in this case sand of the hardest quality. Indeed, unlike the usual notion of carving, it is a process of abrasion and polishing. Various types of sand are used, depending on the hardness, and it is often referred to as jade-cutting-sand (*che yü sha*). Other tools, of steel—wheel, saw, and drill—are also used in the lapidary process but merely to drive the jade-cutting-sand. For example, in dividing a large piece of jade, the saw is applied by moving it back and forth against the jade with the abrasive agent of the sand-and-water mixture. Of course, the saw is toothless, merely a piece of metal. Consequently, in the process of modifying the jade, whether in shaping, engraving and open-work decor, or perforation, there is involved the same or similar abrasive process of using the jade-cutting-sand.

It is obvious that such a working process is time-consuming and calls for great skill. Good craftsmanship demands skill not only in shaping and modifying the raw material but also in using the material sensitively as a means of artistic expression. Often it is the very virtuosity of the craftsmanship that brings the artistic, sometimes hidden, potential of the jade to its fullest materialization—a beautiful art object. For example, in the National Palace Museum in Taiwan, Republic of China, there is a white jade (jadeite) Chinese cabbage (Ch'ing Dynasty, A.D. 1644–1911); the jade itself contains white, green, and tints of red. The artist ingeniously transformed the jade into a natural-looking Chinese cabbage by utilizing each of these inherent color variations in depicting the parts of the cabbage: green leaves, white stems, and tinted reddish root. Thus, it is the combination of human effort and the natural beauty of the stone that brings forth the final realization of a satisfying and exciting work of art.

It is for the above three reasons that jade objects are to be appreciated as one of man's favorite and most highly regarded objects of art. It is a pity, however, that conservative scholars who make a study of Chinese jade tend to pay more attention to ancient jade. The truth is, the value of ancient Chinese jade has been well recognized, but the new and modern (after the Han Dynasty, ca. A.D. 220) jade objects are just as valuable and fascinating.

Art continues to progress and flourish until it is no longer favored by the people. For example, during the Shang (ca. 1766–1122 B.C.) and Chou (ca. 1122–221 B.C.) eras in China, the bronze industry achieved its artistic zenith which even twentieth-century manufacture could not surpass. The decline is not a matter of technology or artistic sensibility, but simply the fact that the art of creating bronze objects is no longer the most important. However, the situation with the art of Chinese jade carving is different as it has survived throughout China's entire history and continues to attract considerable attention. Naturally, the technique and craftsmanship of jade lapidary have improved tremendously in the course of time, and artistic excellence has inevitably been achieved. Outstanding, perhaps, is the manifestation of jade craftsmanship during the Ch'ing Dynasty (A.D. 1644–1911), Ch'ien Lung's reign (ca A.D. 1736–1795) in particular, which surpasses that of all previous times, and measuring from a pure aesthetic point of view, one is forced to acknowledge its great artistic significance.

Indeed, the collection of Dr. J. J. Schedel, emphasizing mainly jade objects from the Ming (ca. A.D. 1368–1644) and Ch'ing (A.D. 1644–1911) dynasties, presents some of the most exquisite examples for the study, understanding, and enjoyment of modern and recent * jade craftsmanship in China.

Na Chi-liang
November 12, 1973
National Palace Museum
Taiwan, Republic of China

Translation by Vera Shu-Ning Sun
*Chinese history considers all dynasties, from the Han Dynasty, A.D. 220, to today, modern and recent history.

CHINESE DYNASTIES

HSIA . . . . (Legendary ? –1766 B.C.)

SHANG . . . . 1766–1122 B.C.

CHOU . . . . 1122–221 B.C.

CH'IN . . . . 221–206 B.C.

HAN . . . . 206 B.C.–A.D. 220

THREE KINGDOMS . . . . A.D. 220–280

SIX DYNASTIES 280–589

SUI 589–618

T'ANG 618–908

FIVE DYNASTIES 908–960

SUNG 960–1279

YÜAN 1260–1368

MING 1368–1644

CH'ING 1644–1911

REPUBLIC 1912–

COLLECTING CHINESE JADE

Invariably people ask me why I collect old jade and how I acquired the desire to do so. My early interest was probably motivated when, as a young boy, I talked to one of my father's employees who had just returned from the Boxer Rebellion. Then, during my public school years, our family lived in Munich, Germany, and our school classes made frequent educational visits to the many art museums of the city. During these visits I gradually became imbued with love for ancient art, especially Oriental art.

Jade particularly fascinated me because these artifacts really are the history of the old China, with its palaces, temples, and its Forbidden City in Peking. The carvings are beautifully executed, with the artist revealing his knowledge and artistry of the raw material available. He must have imagination to take advantage of the various physical aspects, such as the shape of the piece of jade he is carving, and the various color combinations which must be integrated into the design, ranging from pure white to every shade of green, blue, and yellow.

Today prices seem fantastic, but even in the old days the relation between earnings and cost never was much different. In my younger years I thought it improbable that some day I could acquire my own collection.

On my occasional trips to Europe, Australia, and the Orient, I always visited shops showing antiques and gradually acquired knowledge of how to examine an object. I always carry a ten-power magnifying glass. Often a piece has been repaired so cleverly that even a magnifying glass does not reveal the damage; however, it can readily be detected under an ultraviolet light.

In 1944 I purchased my first carving of jade sculpture, Plate 82, a pair of spinach-green birds of paradise. While they are of poor quality, they are kept in the collection as a memento. Then I went to Hong Kong and from there to Taiwan and Tokyo, returning to these places several times, and after a diligent search of the stores, managed to purchase a few pieces. I have acquired some pieces at auction and from many private collectors. Beware of the auction sales, as some have notoriously bad reputations. In purchasing at auction I always examine the desired piece carefully beforehand in daylight, then I make up my mind as to how much I will pay for the article and let the auctioneer know my intention. Invariably I close the bargain at my price.

Very little jade that is older than 1850 is available today. Occasionally a former State Department official who has served prior to Communist take-over in China has authentic artifacts and is willing to part with them.

Every piece is an original and cannot be copied because each piece of raw jade is different. If a similar stone could be found and an artist to carve it, it would be just as valuable as the first piece. Many copies have been made of the same design, but most of these are not jade but lesser hard stones or sometimes only soft soapstone.

Today people purchase many modern porcelain pieces showing birds and other animals, at high prices. The collector buys so-called limited editions, admitting there are others with exactly the same composition. Porcelain is easily damaged, whereas jade is substantial and is broken only with violent action. A psychoanalyst would likely call my desire to own a unique artifact an inferiority complex, but anyone must admit that to own a beautiful statuette which cannot be duplicated imparts great personal satisfaction.

During the time when it was prohibited to bring imports from Communist China into the United States, many objects of jade were sold to Europe and Japan. In fact, original carvings were so depleted in China that the government declared all art objects older than fifty years national property. Today all such articles are sold only by the national government. Due to our embargo, all opportunity to possess untold art objects was lost, and these are now domiciled in other countries and can be acquired only by paying prices sometimes at an increase of 1000 per cent.

No one can be 100 per cent accurate in identifying old objects. Many museums have purchased expensive paintings and later found them to be fakes. While in Sydney, Australia, I was invited to inspect an offering of jade at the dispersal of an estate as the owner was returning to England. He showed me jade pieces which he stated were unsurpassed in excellence, but even a casual inspection proved the material to be ordinary green quartz.

Often the seller shows Certificates of Origin, but "buyer beware," because the certificate is not any better than the issuer. My father used to say, "Paper is patient."

When I occasionally show my jade collection to a visitor, invariably the standard response is, "But I thought jade was green." The fact is that jade is found in almost any variation of color. The shades are entirely dependent upon the presence of infinitesimal amounts of various mineral components, such as iron, cobalt, chrome.

The name "jade" is usually applied to two mineral combinations, nephrite (silicate of magnesium) and jadeite (silicate of aluminum). Nephrite is fibrous material and has a hardness factor of $5\frac{1}{2}$ to $6\frac{1}{2}$ and a specific gravity of 2.90 to 3.02. Jadeite is of crystalline formation with a hardness factor of $6\frac{1}{2}$ to 7 and a specific gravity of 3.30 to 3.36. In comparison, diamonds have a hardness factor of 10 and gypsum of 2.

Nephrite was polished to a dull gloss, and from this the term "mutton fat" was derived. Jadeite finishes with bright high-gloss colors.

There is a third mineral designated as chloromelanite which is also classified as jade and is rarely encountered. Its specific gravity is 3.4, hardness $6\frac{1}{2}$ to 7. It is a black variety of jade obtained in Burma. Today many articles are sold under catchnames, such as Taiwan Jade, Jasper Jade, Su-chou Jade. The novice collector should not be misled, as many of these objects are made of lesser hard stones, such as serpentine, bowenite, obsidian, aventurine; occasionally they are made of ordinary soapstone. The best advice is, if there is a doubt, forget it. But if you find the object interesting prior to purchasing, submit it to one of the many testing laboratories for positive identification.

Most of the older objects are made of nephrite. Jadeite carvings first appeared in China during the last half of the eighteenth century. The rough stones are found among the gravel of rivers, or it is mined in the mountains of Turkistan. The best jadeite is found in Burma, with some deposits extending into adjoining Chinese territories. Jade has been found in many countries, but these deposits always have proved limited and unsuitable for carving. The old deposits are all nearly exhausted, and as the demand is growing, prices naturally increase. Lately jade pieces have been sold at prices rivaling the cost of old master paintings.

Various objects are carved from the rough stone. The archaic pieces of jade are of archaeological importance, and from them we can trace the entire history of the territory we commonly call China. It appears that no matter who conquered this territory and ruled it for a period, jade was always desired and revered. Most of the jade objects originating before and during the Han Dynasty (206 B.C. to A.D. 220) were recovered from burial sites. The belief was that when a body was buried with all apertures closed with a piece of jade, the dormant soul could not escape and jade would prevent putrefaction.

Originally all jade carvings were created with very primitive tools, such as iron wire saws drawn by two men and grinding wheels operated by foot-powered treadles. Grinding media were sand, garnet, other silicates. The work was slow and tedious. While the objects are carvings, they actually were produced by a grinding process. Later, as the art progressed, corundum and carborundum were used as grinding media.

During the later dynasties each emperor had his own factory employing many carvers. At the beginning of the twentieth century power-driven tools gradually came into use. Pieces produced by these means are easily recognized, as the corners of decorations, such as meanders in old pieces, are sharp and those cut with mechanical tools often overlap. Also, curved engravings are not as smooth and uniform. These flaws are due chiefly to the fact that the speed of the mechanical cutting wheels is not so easily stopped as that of foot-operated treadles.

It is difficult to determine the approximate age of the carved object, although clues to the age are generally evident in the repetitions of the various symbols and decoration. Also, the style of the carving denotes the approximate period; however, during the Ch'ien Lung regime many motifs were copied from ancient bronzes. Religious periods also had their influence on the artist. Certain types of meanders, masques, or other engravings are associated with certain eras.

At the present time a great deal of archaic exploration is under way in China. As a result a closer relationship between hearsay and actual fact may be established.

Previous to the Boxer Rebellion in 1900 very little jade was exported. Not only did the warring parties cause much destruction but many jade objects were stolen and found their way to the European market. The same was true during and after the 1912 Civil War which created the republic.

Age is not always the governing factor in the purchase of an addition to the collection. The prime consideration is the beauty of the workmanship. Second is the quality of stone and the artist's interpretation of the various colors and wavy variegations inherent in the rough material. Also the utilization of these qualities.

Many books and articles have been written expounding details, and the novice collector would do well to read several of these, which are readily available in libraries and bookstores. Visiting various known collections in the museums is also a means of education in the art of jade.

My collection consists primarily of objects of newer dynasties. The Chinese people looked upon their rulers with great reverence. A carver's ambition was to have his ruler, whether mandarin, prince, or emperor, choose one of his creations. It was considered an insult to his master if the carver signed his own name to his work. Whenever the object went into the household of the emperor, his seal would then be engraved on the piece, usually on the bottom of the base of the sculpture.

LIST OF PLATES

SHANG DYNASTY—1766–1122 B.C.
CHOU DYNASTY—1122–221 B.C.

Most of the surviving jades of these periods are ritual carvings used in religious ceremonies and symbolizing objects of reverence and adoration. The principal emblems were as follows:

The oldest of these objects were called PI, rendering homage to Heaven. This is a round tablet with a round hole in the center, and a good example is the jade decoration shown in Plate 95. Next in order came the Ts'ung, generally made of yellow-and-brown nephrite, rendering homage to earth and made with a square cross-section. The cylinder is carved through the entire length of the object so it appears as a tube open on each end in the form of a circle within a square. There is a great variation in size, color, and proportion. Chronologically following the PI and Ts'ung are the Kuei, Tae Chang, the Hu, and Huang.

Plates 1 and 2

This Ts'ung is a good example of ritual carving made of yellow-and-brown nephrite.

One side of the object has an engraved text written in archaic Chinese (Plate 2). Not all the characters in the archaic inscription are identifiable. The approximate translation appears with the plate.

Rectangular: 8⅛ × 8⅜ in.
             (20.6 × 21.22 cm.)
Height: 6⅜ in.
       (16.19 cm.)
Inside diameter of cylinder: approximately 6¾ in.
               (17.14 cm.)

Weight: 16½ pounds

Plate 2

"In the first month King Ten Temple of Chou ordered to make vessels to record and to celebrate good virtues [or deeds] in temples. In use for ten thousand endless years and in perpetuity by sons and grandsons."

During the later years of the Han emperors the first contact was probably made with the West. Indian Buddhism was introduced, and with it new ideas were developed by jade carvers. In later centuries these ideas were gradually expanded. The following four hundrd years show little improvement as the country was in continuous turmoil due to civil wars and Tartar invasions. This period is designated as the Six Dynasties. The T'ang Dynasty was established in A.D. 618 and prevailed until A.D. 908. From this time on, less jade was buried with the dead and more was preserved for the living and then handed down for posterity either by the conqueror or by subsequent princes. During this regime carving became more defined and many artifacts were made for personal adornment. It was an age of recovery of past artistry, and it set the basis of accomplishment and standard of imitation for future dynasties. Innumerable small animal carvings were created, many in dark and black jade. Good carvings of this period are rare.

HAN DYNASTY

Plate 3

Dark nephrite libation cup with an animal form handle in the almost abstract style that is so typical of the period. Notice the similarity to the dancing figures from the same period. Although this piece is done in jade, there is the same sophisticated, simplified style that marks this one of the artistic high points of the archaic period.

Nephrite—1⅞ in. diameter × 2 in. high
$\quad$ (4.8 × 5.08 cm.)

Figure of Fo Dog from the Han period. The bulk and force of the piece forecast the later Ming pieces and have a similar feeling.

Nephrite—2½ × 1½ × 1⅞ in., including wood base.
$\quad$ (6.3 × 3.8 × 4.8 cm.)

T'ANG DYNASTY

Plate 4

Dromedary camel with young. Celadon-green-and-brown nephrite. While classified T'ang, this piece could be much older.

3¼ in. long × 1⅝ in. wide × 1¼ in. high
(8.25 × 4.1 × 3.2 cm.)

Elongated dog sleeping. Sculptured from yellow-greenish nephrite.

2⅜ in. long × ¾ in. wide × 1⅜ in. high
(6.0 × 1.9 × 3.5 cm.)

Plate 5

Goatlike mythical animal carved from celadon-green-and-brown nephrite. This piece may have been used as an amulet by threading a silk cord through a round hole made by the horns.

2 in. long × ⅞ in. wide × 1⅝ in. high
(5.08 × 2.2 × 4.1 cm.)

Mythical temple lion carved from yellow-brown nephrite. Feet have three claws, and in bottom are two holes showing this piece may have been a body ornament fastened with a silk cord.

1¾ in. long × 1 in. wide × 1⅜ in. high
(4.5 × 2.54 × 3.5 cm.)

SUNG DYNASTY—A.D. 960–1279

During the Sung Dynasty carvings showed an advancement in details. A number of small animal statues were carved from yellowish-brown nephrite. The carvings were more delicate and graceful in form. During this time there appeared larger and bolder types of libation cups and bowls. Some of these had dragon or phoenix bird motifs. Also, interest was shown in the copying of ancient bronzes.

During the last year of the Sung Dynasty, art prospered, and with it religious philosophy and confrontations flourished at the same time. However, there was a deterioration of military power, and the country was an easy prey to the onrushing Mongols.

Plate 6

Water buffalo exquisitely carved from a black-and-variegated-gray piece of nephrite. This is the most perfectly carved small object in my collection. The artist took advantage of the variegations and veinlets.

2½ in. long × 1⅜ in. wide × 1 in. high
(6.3 × 3.5 × 2.54 cm.)

Tigerlike sleeping animal. Carved from black-and-white nephrite. A beautifully executed smooth carving. Drilled for suspension on a silk cord.

2¼ in. long × 1⅛ in. wide × 1 in. high
(5.7 × 2.9 × 2.54 cm.)

Elongated dog resting, made of dark-brown nephrite. Excellent carving and smooth finish.

2¾ in. long × 1 in. wide × 1 in. high
(7.0 × 2.54 × 2.54 cm.)

Plate 7

Stylized turtle with goat head sitting on a base. An uncommon combination formed from a dark brown spotted piece of nephrite. Carving on sides of the platform are typical meanders.
Drilled for ornamental suspension.

1⅞ in. square—1½ in. high
(4.8 × 4.8 × 3.8 cm.)

Small frog, in sitting position, showing alertness. Good carving of yellow-and-brown nephrite.

1⅞ in. long × 1⅜ in. wide × 1 in. high
(4.8 × 3.5 × 2.54 cm.)

Dagger hilt made of brown-white nephrite. Front shows a Hydra (dragonlike sea serpent). Back shows tao-teh masque.

1⅞ in. long × ⅝ in. wide × ⅞ in. high
(4.8 × 1.6 × 2.2 cm.)

Plate 8

Mythical unicorn monster of yellow-brown nephrite. Reverse side shows a typical wing of a chimera or guardian of the temple. The feet are five-toed, typical of the Imperial Dragon, and the right front foot rests on the great Pearl.

2⅜ in. long × 1⅜ in. wide × 1¾ in. high
(6.0 × 3.5 × 4.5 cm.)

Horse, in reclining position, sculptured from yellow-and-brown nephrite. The artist fully anticipated the variegations of the rough stone.

2⅜ in. long × 1⅛ in. wide × 1⅝ in. high
(6.0 × 2.9 × 4.1 cm.)

Temple dog, in sitting position, made of celadon-and-brown nephrite.

2 in. long × 1 in. wide × 1⅞ in. high
(5.08 × 2.54 × 4.8 cm.)

Plate 9

Feline animal of celadon nephrite with brown face. Small round hole is drilled through the body, and this piece probably was used as a charm hanging on a silk cord.

2⅜ in. × ¾ in. × 1 in.
(6.0 × 1.9 × 2.54 cm.)

Tiger scratching behind ear. Made of celadon-green-and-brown spotted nephrite. Probably a suspension ornament.

2¾ in. long × 2 in. wide × 1 in. high
(7.0 × 5.08 × 2.54 cm.)

Water buffalo reclining, with boy grooming or washing the animal. Light green nephrite with black rind material.

3¼ in. long × 1⅝ in. wide × 1⅞ in. high
(8.25 × 4.1 × 4.8 cm.)

YÜAN DYNASTY—A.D. 1260–1368

The Mongol Empire lasted a comparatively short time. Jade development was at a standstill, and only a few pieces survived. Most of these show a distinct aura of dignity, as in Plate 10.

Its best-known emperors were the notorious conquerors Kublai and Genghis Khan and Tamerlane.

Plate 10

Dark moss-green carving of a Mandarin deity. Most unusual, since it is from the Yüan Dynasty, from which very few pieces have been preserved. The strict simplicity and matte finish are both typical of the period.

There is an almost "modern" feeling in this piece, as there is no superfluous decoration, and the strength of the man and his period come through clearly.

With carved wooden chair.

Nephrite—9 × 4½ × 3¼ in.
      (22.86 × 11.43 × 8.25 cm.)

MING DYNASTY—A.D. 1368–1644

After the fall of the Mongol emperors the Ming Dynasty arrived in China and the art of jade carving again became a major development. Many archaic bronzes were copied in jade. A new style became apparent, with bolder and more positive lines showing strength and purpose. A good example is Plate 16. Favorite subjects were water buffalo and horses. The artifacts were larger, encrusted with Fo Dogs, Hydras, and dragons.

During the sixteenth century the finest pieces of the Ming period were created. Elaborate relief forms decorated the altar vessels and cups. However, history repeated itself. The country was prosperous and weakened its defenses, and the Manchus conquered.

Plate 11

Excellent carving of reclining horse with monkey currying its back. In mottled black nephrite.

2⅜ in. long × ¾ in. wide × 1¼ in. high
(6.0 × 1.9 × 3.2 cm.)

Short-legged Mongolian pony with typical Ming head. Sculptured of yellow-brown nephrite. Base finished with a wavelike pattern.

2½ in. long × ⅝ in. wide × 1¼ in. high
(6.3 × 1.6 × 3.2 cm.)

Beautifully executed mythical animal with three clawed feet and bi-fold tail. In brown-and-brownish-white nephrite. Artist took full advantage of the two-tone coloration of the rough stone. With hole for suspension.

2¼ in. long × ¾ in. wide × 1⅛ in. high
(5.7 × 1.9 × 2.9 cm.)

Plate 12

Lin deer resting. Made of two-tone white-and-brownish nephrite. Rare square hole is carved through body; evidently carving was used as an amulet.
The lin deer is an emblem of good luck.

3 in. long × ⅝ in. wide × 1¼ in. high
(7.62 × 1.6 × 3.2 cm.)

Sleeping dog with young. White-and-brown mottled nephrite tails curved in typical Ming fashion. Suspension ornament.

2⅞ in. long × 1⅜ in. wide × ⅞ in. high
(7.3 × 3.5 × 2.2 cm.)

Long-horned reclining ram made of white nephrite.

2⅝ in. long × ⅞ in. wide × 1½ in. high
(6.7 × 2.2 × 3.8 cm.)

Plate 13

Reclining ram. Very plain in greenish-brown nephrite.

2½ in. long × 1 in. wide × 1½ in. high
(6.3 × 2.54 × 3.8 cm.)

Superbly executed carving of elephant. Light green nephrite with black striping. The ornamental drape is engraved with a winding flowery design and cloud pattern. Chinese appearance.

2¾ in. long × 1¼ in. wide × 1⅞ in. high
(7.0 × 3.2 × 4.8 cm.)

Plate 14

Scene depicts Buddha, with two attendants, sitting in Court of Judgment comprised of Eighteen Lohans (similar to the Apostles of the Christian religion). Tribunal is sitting in judgment of a mythological monkey who became very powerful but had abused his privileges. Buddha was supreme, and the monkey feared his power would be taken away.
The reverse side shows a garden scene with fish in the water and a bird on the swing basket (signifying heavenly surplus). Early Ming period with typical waxy finish. Yellow-and-green jade with boulder "skin" of rust red.

Nephrite—8½ × 4½ × 4 in.
         (21.59 × 11.43 × 10.16 cm.)
Hung Wu period—A.D. 1368–1398

Plate 15

Sculpture in gray-green color with black intrusions represents Fo Lion in reclining position. The geometrical patterns of the head carving appear similar to those of the Chou period.
This piece was probably created during the early Ming Dynasty. Weight is eight pounds.

Nephrite—9 in. long × 4⅜ in. wide × 3 in. high
(22.86 × 11.11 × 7.62 cm.)

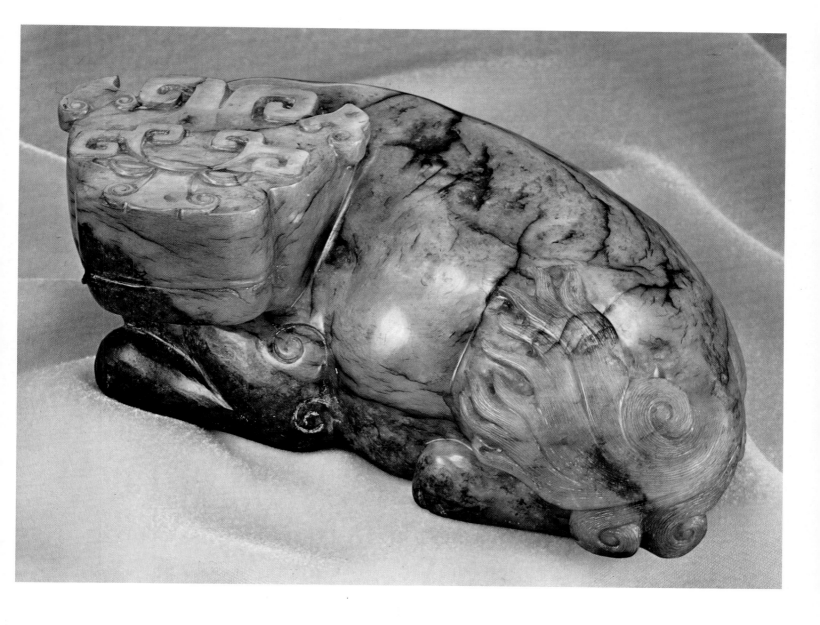

Plates 16 and 17

Rare blue-gray horse. Unusually fine carving and detail masterfully accomplished, expressing the mass and strength of the Ming period style.

Again, as in Plate 21, notice the strong spine line and the very literal delineation of all the body parts. Flowing curves contrast strongly with definite lines and strong characterization, especially in the head. Many pieces of this period seem to have an unnatural position, especially in the neck and head.

Note the beautifully carved undermembers (Plate 17).

With carved wooden base.

Nephrite—7 × 5 × 3¾ in.
        (17.78 × 12.70 × 9.52 cm.)
Probably sixteenth century

Plate 17

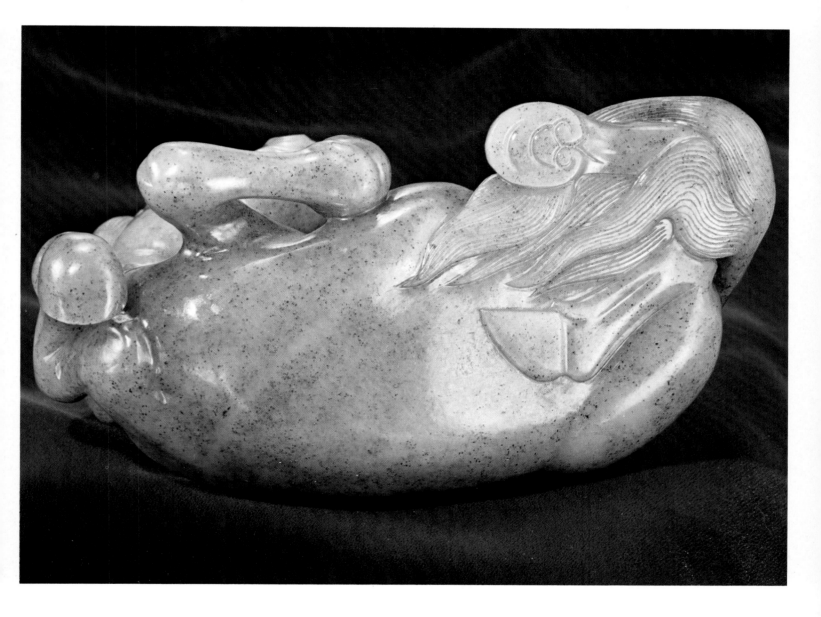

Plate 18

Typical Ming period execution of polish identifies this piece as a copy of archaic bronze of Hsia, Shang, and Chou periods.
The dragon tongue holds a loose ring. The dragon masque comprises the spout from which sweep teeth and power bands signifying clouds and thunder. Four feet depict mythological phoenix birds. The handle is a stylized dragon. The urn stands on a solid wood base.

Nephrite—7⅛ × 8⅞ × 3½ in.
(18.10 × 22.54 × 8.89 cm.)
Wan Li period—A.D. 1573–1619

Plate 19

Recumbent figure of a water buffalo in dark celadon-green jade with inclusions of brown jade "skin." The massive quality of the animal suggests the Ming period. During this period the subject reached its peak of popularity. The finish suggests a possible repolishing because of its high gloss; however, the carving is typical of the period.

Throughout many centuries jade carvers have immortalized the Chinese esteem for the buffalo or ox, which according to many authorities is considered to have emanated from a regard for the animal as an emblematic symbol of spring and agriculture. Others favor the later belief that it was, in fact, held by the early Chinese to be their River God.

With wooden stand.

Nephrite—7½ × 5¼ × 3 in.
(19.05 × 13.33 × 7.62 cm.)
Wan Li period—A.D. 1573–1619

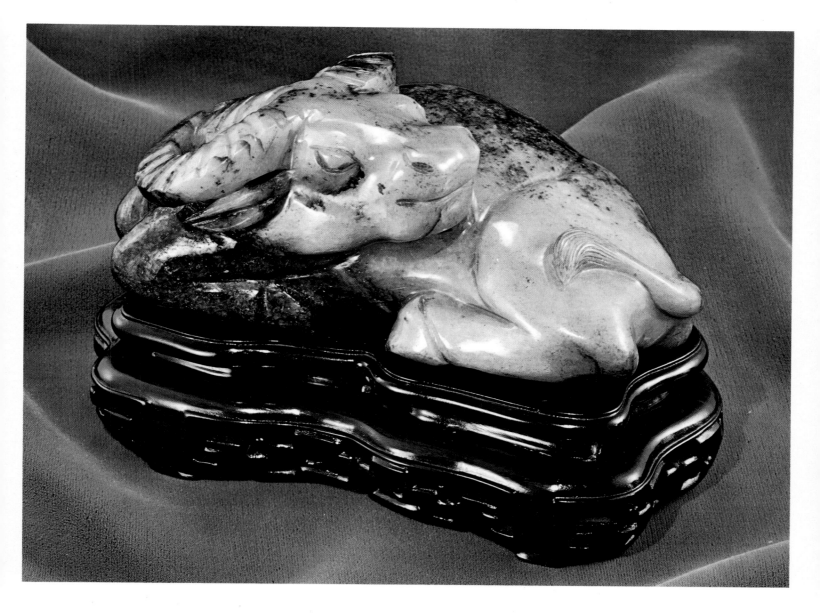

Plate 20

Important brown-and-white hand-carved jade Chimera with blunt nose, his wings folded against his body, with head resembling that of a Fo Lion; pointed ears, and lips curled, showing his teeth. The surface evinces the even waxiness of all Ming jade pieces.

It was the special duty of the Chimera to guard all gates. He was the equivalent of Janus in Roman mythology. Qualities of mass and power, so highly developed during the Ming period, are brilliantly shown in this awesome carving.

Nephrite—5¼ × 3¼ × 7¼ in.
        (13.33 × 8.25 × 18.41 cm.)
Ch'ung Cheng period—A.D. 1628–1643

Plate 21

Recumbent mare with half-seated foal, its front feet and shoulders resting on its mother's back. In unusual tones of red, brown, and cream jade, executed in Ming style, and dating from that period.

This is one of the most commonly copied subjects from the Ming period. The collector should take careful note of the strong line of the spine of the mare and the sharp definition and delineation of all body members, especially the broad, flat nose plane and the clear carving of all the hair in the manes and tails.

With fitted carved stand.

Nephrite—4¾ × 7⅛ ×3½ in.
        (12.06 × 18.10 × 8.89 cm.)
Ch'ung Cheng period—A.D. 1628–1643

Plate 22

This is one of the finest sculptures in my collection. Superb carving, especially in the execution of horses' tails. Also, the mane shows tremendous understanding by the artist. Amazingly natural is the stance of the mare and colt. Notice the fetlocks.
Natural variation of the rock is cleverly exploited to show striping of the subject. The finish is satin smooth, the color white with a slight tint of sea green.

Nephrite—7 in. long × 4½ in. wide × 5 in. high
(17.78 × 11.43 × 12.7 cm.)
Probably first half of the sixteenth century

CH'ING DYNASTY—A.D. 1644–1911

In A.D. *1644 the Ming emperors were overthrown by the Ch'ing conquerors. The Manchu Dynasty lasted until the creation of the Republic of China in 1912. Ch'ien Lung, the fourth Manchu emperor, reigned from* A.D. *1736 until 1795. He was a great lover of the arts. Jade carving reached its zenith of perfection. The carvings became masterpieces of art portraying koros (incense burners), delicate carved mountain scenes, statues of Buddha, of the Eight Immortals of deities and queens. Vessels, such as cups and flower vases, were produced. It is doubtful that the bowls and cups were used as cooking utensils, but certainly they were used on the altars of the temples during religious ceremonies.*

The Emperor Ch'ien Lung was also a poet, and on some of the jades of his time poems of the emperor were inscribed. This is more often found on the reverse side of mountain pieces, and the poem is often the description of the scenery shown. A good example is Plate 44.

During the later years of Ch'ien Lung, jadeite appeared in quantity from the Burma deposits and some of the most colorful artifacts were produced. Good examples of these products are Plates 65 and 70. So-called Tibetan-type carvings show the Lamaistic influence. These objects, mainly incense burners and perfume bowls, have a style of their own. Special features are openwork, where the shell is pierced, instead of surface decorations. A good specimen is Plate 57.

K'ANG HSI PERIOD—A.D. 1662–1722

Plate 23

Perfectly carved resting water buffalo. Note the lead rope made of rare honey-colored nephrite.

2⅞ in. long × 1⅛ in. wide × 1⅝ in. high
(7.3 × 2.9 × 4.1 cm.)

Plate 24

Group of three goats carved of sea-green nephrite. Nuzzling fungus of Immortality.

2½ in. long × 1¼ in. wide × 1⅜ in. high
(6.3 × 3.2 × 3.5 cm.)

White statue of one of the Eight Immortals. Reverse is of carved brown rind of original stone. Small Fo Dog is beside main figure.

1⅝ in. long × ⅞ in. wide × 3 in. high
(4.1 × 2.2 × 7.62 cm.)

Horse resting made of sea-green nephrite. Drilled for suspension.

1⅞ in. long × 1 in. wide × 1 in. high
(4.8 × 2.54 × 2.54 cm.)

Plate 25

Pair of fine Jui (scepters) used in the Imperial court of K'ang Hsi as symbols of rank and power. Unusual as, in all their length, the color is unchanged. Quality of homogeneity and clarity is rare in jade pieces this large. Both pieces were carved from the same boulder.
Decorations are mirror-carved with the subject being exactly reversed from one scepter to the other.

Nephrite—17½ in. long × ⅜ in. thick
      (44.45 × 0.95 cm.)
      Large decoration—5⅛ × 4⅛ in.
               (13.02 × 10.48 cm.)
      Small decoration—2½ × 2¾ in.
               (6.3 × 7.0 cm.)

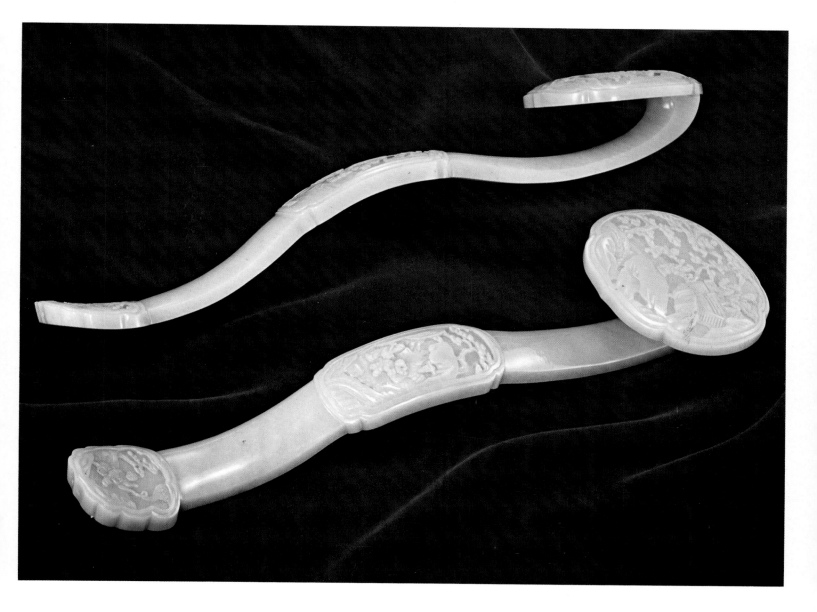

Plate 26

Covered bowl of finest light celadon jade. The handles are exquisitely carved peony flowers and leaves. Each handle has a loose ring. The cover depicts a four-toed dragon (Mandarin). This bowl was used as an incense burner.

Nephrite—6¼ × 6¼ in.
(15.87 × 15.87 cm.)

CH'IEN LUNG PERIOD—A.D. 1736–1795

Plate 27

Horse with monkey made of black-and-white nephrite. Suspension piece.

1⅞ in. long × ⅝ in. wide × 1⅝ in. high
(4.8 × 1.6 × 4.1 cm.)

Pig resting. Made of interesting black nephrite.

2¼ in. long × 1¼ in. wide × ¾ in. high
(5.7 × 3.2 × 1.9 cm.)

Plate 28

Squirrel-like animal sitting on top of a melon covered with leaves. Made of white nephrite interspersed with brown areas. Two butter-flies shown in carving.

2⅝ in. long × 1⅜ in. wide × 2 in. high
(6.7 × 3.5 × 5.08 cm.)

Two weasel-like animals entwined, made of white-and-brown nephrite. Suspension piece.

1½ in. long × 1¼ in. wide × 1½ in. high
(3.8 × 3.2 × 3.8 cm.)

Plate 29

Two figurines of the eighteenth century carved from exquisite yellow jade represent the "Matchmakers": Golden Boy and Jade Beauty Girl. Chinese custom provides that parents consult Matchmakers to select mates for their children. In early China children were betrothed at an infantile age. The Golden Boy was to select the girl, and the Jade Beauty Girl recommended the boy for betrothal.

Yellow jade is the rarest of all colors and considered premium pieces of the collection.

With wooden bases.

Nephrite—3⅛ in. high × 1⅜ in. long × 1 in. wide
(7.93 × 3.5 × 2.54 cm.)

Plate 30

Gray-white vase of typical Han Shane carved during the reign of Ch'ien Lung. Unusual iris carvings in handle with free-carved rings. The basic Ku form has been decorated with panels running perfectly, top to bottom, in serrated planes. Hibiscus flowers, which hold the free ring carvings, indicate the Lamaistic influence of Buddhist art forms.

Nephrite—10⅝ in. high × 5⅝ in. long × 4½ in. wide
(26.99 × 14.22 × 11.43 cm.)

Plate 31

Vase is of pure white jade of the finest and rarest quality. Sides show dragon masques in fine bas-relief. Unusual elephant head handles with trunks holding loose ring carvings. Vines hold two more loose rings in the finial.

Rarity and purity of color make this a valuable and highly desirable piece.

With wooden stand.

Nephrite—5 in. $\times$ 3⅜ in. $\times$ 1⅝ in.
            (12.70 $\times$ 8.57 $\times$ 4.1 cm.)

Plate 32

This carving is a depiction of the bravery and cleverness of the Lady Liang, wife of a general of the Ming period. When the battle seemed to be going badly, in order to confuse the enemy, she beat a drum at several locations on the battlefield. Her son (the boy with the flag) accompanied her. The enemy, convinced of the overwhelming number of battle units, withdrew from the field, and the victory went to the general and the clever Lady Liang.

The finish of the piece is fine polish and the color a bright celadon green. One can feel the force of the wind pulling at the flying flag, which is bending the pole and rippling the wavelike edges of the banner.

Nephrite—9⅛ × 7¼ × 2 in.
(23.18 × 18.41 × 5.08 cm.)

Plate 33

Pair of sea-mist-green covered urns. Lotus flowers and foliage with seed pods. Finial is an undercut dragon, which has the four toes of Mandarin rank. Carved bronze form in high relief with loose pendant jade ring handles on each side, with silver inlaid carved wooden stands. Butternut leaves and the meander of the dragon horn are beautifully executed in the most classic style. Lamaistic influence shown by hibiscus blossoms.

Depth of the carving and delicacy of the curvilinear pattern defy even photography. This is a perfect example of the mysterious fascination of jade carving.

Nephrite—14¾ × 6 × 2⅞ in.
 (37.46 × 15.24 × 7.30 cm.)

Plate 34

The three-legged toad bearing a boy on his back is in fine white jade with brilliant emerald-green spots. The three-legged toad is the symbol of good fortune and, according to legend, is supposed to live in the moon.
With carved wooden base.

Nephrite—7 × 5 × 2¼ in.
          (17.78 × 12.70 × 5.7 cm.)

Plate 35

Sea-mist-green jade figure of the Goddess Mei Yin with a lion. The finest example of mass and motion in Chinese jade carving.
The Goddess, with hair piled atop her head, and wearing a long-sleeved robe, holds a flower spray in her right hand, while her left hand rests on an exquisitely carved Fo Lion with a bushy tail.
With flower-carved wooden stand.

Nephrite—11½ × 4¼ × 3 in.
(29.21 × 10.79 × 7.62 cm.)

Plate 36

Magnificent koro of unusually opalescent and luminescent white jade from the period of Ch'ien Lung. The handles are dragon heads with the horns of power; free carved rings are held in the dragons' mouths. The power symbol derives from an archaic delineation of thunder and lightning and is found in all periods of Chinese art. The top has four panels, with dragons surmounted by two Fo Dogs. Purity of color and freedom from inclusion are rarely seen in so large a piece. The carved fitted top has slits for emitting incense fragrance and smoke.

This koro derives its form from the ancient vessel called a ting which, according to certain authorities, was used to hold cooked food on the altar, in the manner of a libation offering, while other writers prefer to believe that its use was actually of a utilitarian type, that of an object in which the food was prepared. Undoubtedly, when the ting was formed in bronze, such uses could possibly apply, but of the vessels of this form made in jade, of which there are examples emanating from all periods, it seems most probable that the Chinese-recorded uses of these objects was the most creditable; that they first were produced as containers of the precious juices, used in the manner of the present-day sauces, for condiment service. This koro comes under the broad heading of incense burner, for which such forms have, since the commencement of the Ch'ing Dynasty, most often been utilized.

The circular ting, with its three legs, symbolized heaven with its three luminaries, the sun, moon, and stars. The incense or perfume burners of later times were sometimes modeled on the lines of the ting, and no doubt the legs would prove useful in keeping the heat from damaging the wooden table on which the burner might be placed.

Nephrite—8¼ × 10½ × 6 in.
(20.96 × 26.67 × 15.24 cm.)

Plate 37

These camphor-white circular bowls have been left unadorned, thereby bringing into effective prominence the superb quality of the jade from which these objects are cut.

This type of bowl was used by the wealthy classes to serve a delicacy made of dried petals of the chrysanthemum flower soaked in wine, the resultant liquid being similar in appearance to tea. It was usually served after the chrysanthemum ritual, which was celebrated during the ninth moon, and after viewing the marvelous display of flowers at that time in full bloom, the party would return to the house of their host and partake of this peculiar tea together with a repast of crabs and *samshu*. This custom would appear to be related to the belief that the chrysanthemum is emblematic of a life of ease and retirement from active official duties.

These are one of the rare instances of pieces being inscribed with household marks. "Signatures" like these usually indicate the owner rather than the maker, and in this case they bear the household mark of the Emperor Ch'ien Lung.

With beautifully carved wooden tablelike bases.

Nephrite—6 × 2⅝ × 2¾ in.
          (15.24 × 6.7 × 7.0 cm.)

Plate 38

The Goddess Kuan-Yin, dressed in a long-sleeved robe and a long head covering, holds a begging cup (bowl signifies humility) with both hands while she sits astride a snarling Fo Lion with bushy mane and tail.

The origin of Kuan-Yin, Goddess of Mercy, is wrapped in the mists of remote antiquity. In early Chinese script she is usually described as of Indian origin and form. It has been suggested, without proof, that Kuan-Yin was actually the Chinese Princess Miao-shen, who lived about 2587 B.C., while others believe her to have been a deity first idolized at about 695 B.C. Some Chinese scholars regard her as a manifestation of the Indo-Tibetan divinity, Avalokitesvara.

There is an interesting theory that was given some public credulity a few years ago—that the Chinese, at the time of the introduction of Buddhism, were divided among themselves, some sects favoring the continuance of the worship of a female divinity, presumably the traditional Princess Miao-shen, or perhaps the mythological Mountain and Dawn Goddess Chun-t'i, others favoring the Buddhistic Avalokitesvara, and that eventually, from these three deities, was evolved, in the person of Kuan-Yin, a goddess satisfying the aspirations of all parties. Her form and type, as represented in glyptic art from the Sung Dynasty to the present day, is familiar to all students of Chinese art.

Some of the finest jade carvings, of Kuan-Yin, were produced during the Ch'ien Lung period.

Soft sea-foam nephrite of unusual mass and power. With carved wooden fitted base.

Nephrite—9 × 6⅝ × 3½ in.
(22.86 × 16.82 × 8.89 cm.)

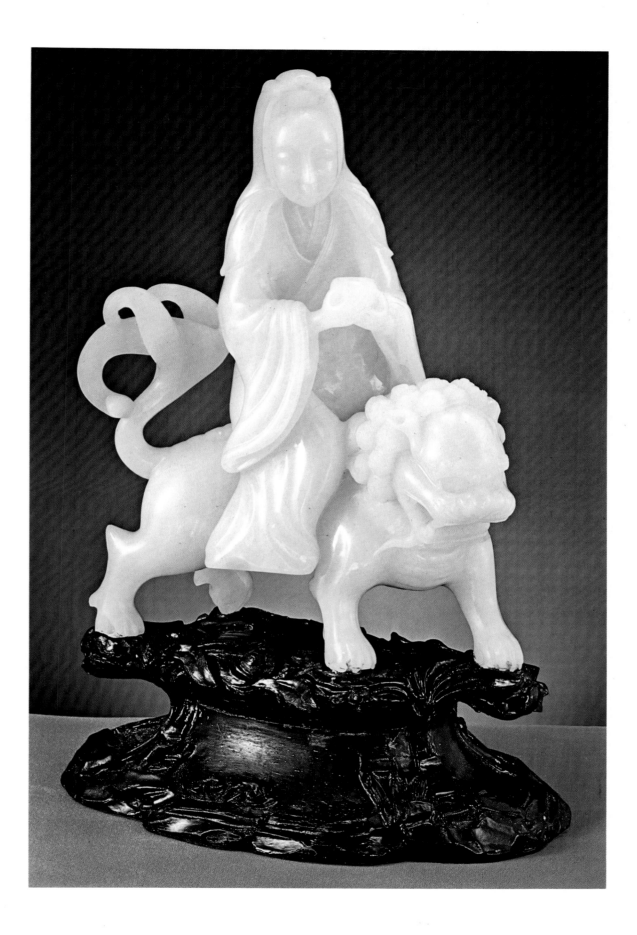

Plates 39 and 40

One of a pair of Ch'ien Lung deeply carved and unusually fine jade screens depicting wilderness scenes in the mountains.

One side displays a monastery that is probably a part of the Summer Palace. It is set under clouds, with bridges, trees, rocks, and waterfalls. The Emperor K'ang Hsi rides a bullock with an attendant and is greeted by the Abbot (former Emperor Shun Chih, father of K'ang Hsi).

The reverse side, Plate 40, shows two lin deer standing in a lush growth of trees, bushes, and foliage, with rocks and paths.

Since the Sung Dynasty, the jade craftsman had embodied in his works the innovation of tree portrayal in a pictorial style. He was possibly influenced by the strong poetic references to the grandeur of tree formations made by the authors of those times and also by an overwhelming desire to express in his works his own innate belief that the regard for trees is not only in and for themselves but is perpetuated and enhanced by their association with other natural elements. This conception, that trees were endowed with special mystic powers, has been exemplified in the manner in which the Chinese have for generations utilized in their arts such subjects as the pine, bamboo, willow, and chestnut.

Each side of the plaque is so unusually carved that, when illuminated from behind, the carving from the opposite side is not visible.

Original finely carved bases of lignum vitae.

Nephrite—9½ in. diameter—½ in. thick
(24.13 × 1.27 cm.)

Plate 40

Plates 41, 42, and 43

Koro of highly translucent spinach-color jade. A magnificently rounded and delicate carving that is so typical of the eighteenth century. Dragon handles are free ring carvings (Plate 42). The finial is of three Lion Dogs(Fo),one of which holds the great Pearl of Happiness(Plate 43). The jade itself is a superb example of the highly prized Siberian nephrite. The piece is signed in seal form with the mark of Ch'ien Lung. The famous Huang Feng (mythical phoenix birds with lion heads) decorate the masterfully carved band on the body of the koro. With base carved of lignum vitae.

Nephrite—8¼ × 8¼ × 5¼ in.
(20.96 × 20.96 × 13.33 cm.)

Plate 42

Plate 43

Plates 44 and 45

This natural boulder carving is an example of crude jade rock being used by the craftsman as the subject of his basic form. The decoration is intricately displayed and very picturesque, including symbolic pine and mulberry trees and the famous Hsueh Pao Waterfall immortalized from very early times in Chinese poetical works. At the bottom of the mountain are three sages, the largest one being, no doubt, Chan-Ya (later canonized as Wen Ch'ang), considered to be the Chinese God of Literature, proceeding to one of his mountain retreats in the vicinity of Such'uan, accompanied by two attendants or possibly other sages. The reverse side, Plate 45, shows waterfalls, with rocks and pines, along with thirty-seven characters in five lines of poetry. Pine trees indicate peace and tranquillity of nature.

It is interesting that the poem on the reverse side, which speaks of the beauty and tranquillity of the scene, also speaks of the instrument carried by the servant, which was especially reserved to be played in just such a scene.

The poem, by the Emperor Ch'ien Lung, is entitled: "Imperial Colophon at Pine Ravine, Visitor Carrying a Ch'in" (stringed musical instrument).

On highly carved wooden stand with sacred fungus and leaf design and open carved areas.

Nephrite—sea mist and yellow—6¾ × 7¾ × 1 in.
(17.14 × 19.68 × 2.54 cm.)

Plate 45

Text of the poem is approximately as follows:
"*Near the running stream and rocky stones, looking far into the sky, responding to each other. Listening the wind under the pines, approaching visitor carrying a ch'in at the edge of the rock, playing chords that bring music in harmony with the beautiful scenery.*"

御製題松磬

攜琴圖

臨流望石昕

長空相答還

聽松下風有

客攜琴來音

口便將動操

韻癊同

Plate 46

This vase is of very delicate sea-mist-green stone. Two phoenix birds stand among branches of Ling Chih, the sacred Fungus of Longevity of the Taoist philosophy. The birds have branches of Ling Chih in their beaks. The carving is of exceptional quality.
Original lignum vitae base mounted on wooden sub-base.

Nephrite—5⅜ in. long × 9 in. high × 1¼ in. wide
(13.65 × 22.86 × 3.2 cm.)

Plate 47

Large perfumer in mottled white and pale rust with domed cover. Elaborately carved and pierced with openwork design of formal scrolling, flowering tree peony branches on flaring base. Heavy loose rings are suspended from openwork flowering peony branch handles.

Nephrite—10¾ in. long × 7¼ in. diameter × 7 in. high
(27.26 × 18.41 × 17.78 cm.)

Plate 48

Bodhisattva formerly of Imperial rank. The complete costume of lace and draperies includes royal and mandarin design. The headdress symbolizes eternity, with begging bowl and bare feet indicating humility.
The intricacy of the tracery designs and the soft flow and layering of the materials mark this piece as suitable to be of Imperial quality. The household mark of the Emperor Ch'ien Lung is incised into the base. Made of unusually clear and pure pale green material.

Nephrite—11½ × 4 × 2¼ in.
(29.21 × 10.16 × 5.7 cm.)

Plate 49

Sea-mist-green vase of early Chou Ku style, with dragons sweeping up from a sea of clouds, with the design continued and completed on the bottom of the vase. From the dragon's mouth comes the cloud bearing rain and the great flaming Pearl of Happiness.

The carving exemplifies the use of archaic style with the addition of contemporary motif of the eighteenth century. The archaic and classic Ku shape is decorated with tao-teh masques and early butternut leaf designs. Dragons come out of an almost timelessly "modern" sea of waves, and the carefully curved lines contrast strongly but beautifully with the strict simplicity of the earlier shape.

Nephrite—9 × 5 × 3⅛ in.
(22.86 × 12.70 × 7.93 cm.)

Plate 50

Perhaps the outstanding of all the nocturnal pieces to be seen, this capped vase of soft sea-mist-green nephrite has an unusually fine clarity and homogeneity of color. Surrounding the main vase shape are figures of the night, and the moon shines over all. The crane indicates purity, the bat and the prunus blossoms indicate fortune and safety, and the deer with the sacred mushroom serenity. The famous "three friends in winter," the pine, plum, and bamboo, indicate that this piece was designed for the festival of the winter season.

Nephrite—12 × 4¾ × 2¼ in.
(30.48 × 12.06 × 5.7 cm.)

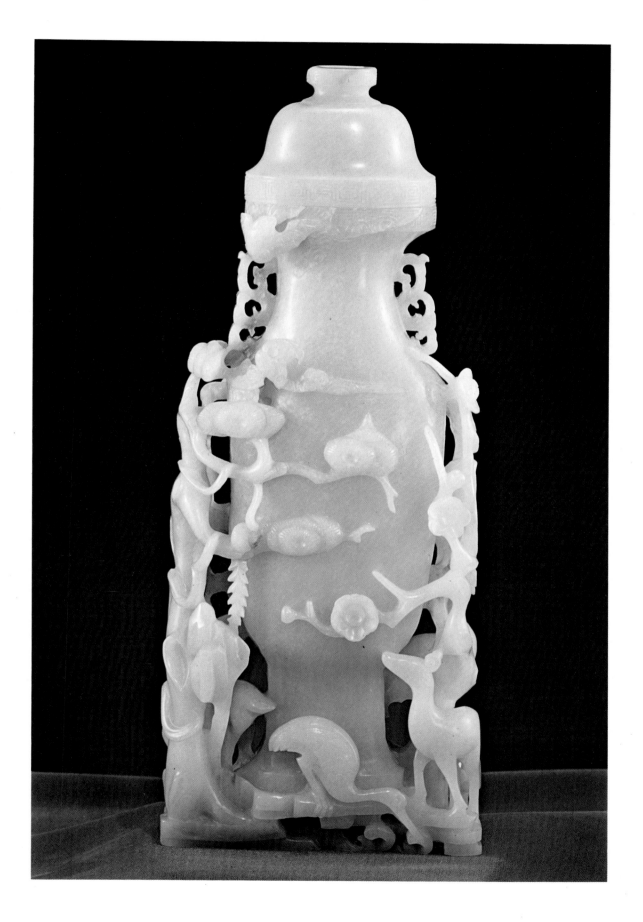

Plate 51

Covered vase of fine white-and-sea-mist-green jade. Cherry tree growing from rocks signifies the results of hard labor in a difficult field,
probably education, indicating the reward of learning.
Again, use of contrasting archaic and eighteenth-century decorative
motif is the keynote of the entire composition (see Plate 49). The
luminosity of jade material is highly prized and seldom found in a
piece of this size.

Nephrite—11 × 5 × 3 in.
        (27.94 × 12.70 × 7.62 cm.)

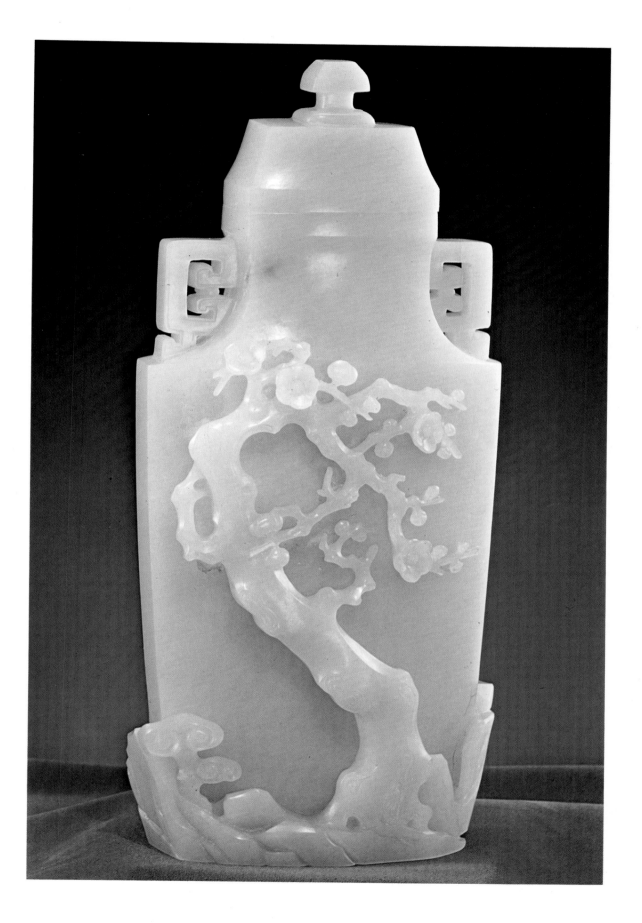

Plate 52

Unusually proportioned mountain of mutton-fat jade. Two philoso-
phers (carrying Lotus Flowers of Immortality) stand over waterfalls
with two lin deer. Tail of the Rain Dragon may be seen in the clouds.
Taste and proportion are excellent, and this is one of the few vertically
treated designs the author has seen.
With carved wooden base.

Nephrite—10 × 4¾ × 2½ in.
          (25.40 × 12.06 × 6.3 cm.)

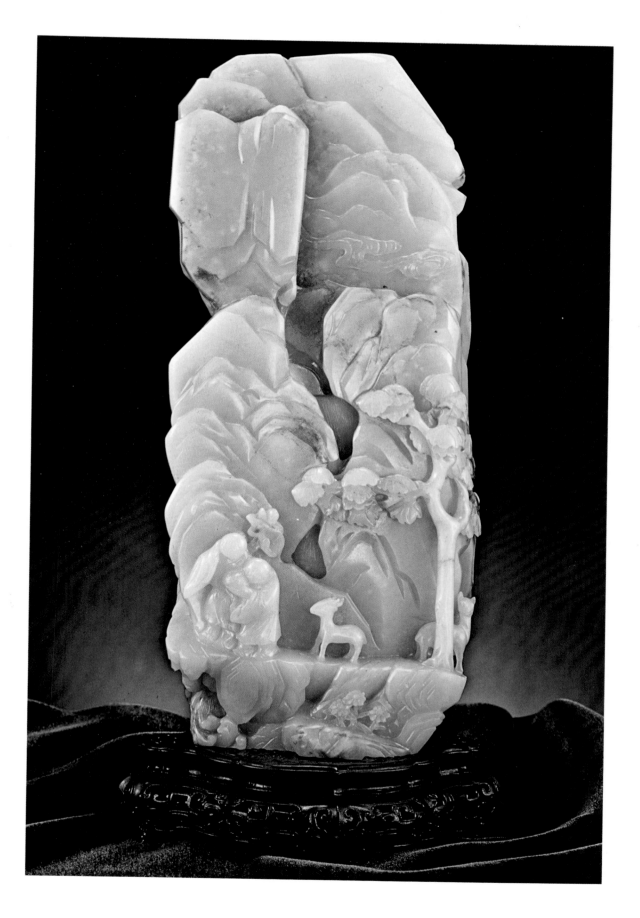

Plate 53

Bowl of light mutton-fat jade with deer's-head handles in full relief and monster masques (bas-relief) in the rim. Cover has masques set in meanders (power symbol of dragon horns) in the archaic (Han) bronze style. Symbols are repeated along the sides of the bowl. Signed in center of bottom of base.

Carvings are typical style of Ch'ien Lung, indicating the great delicacy and perfection of detail which raise this period to its great height. With wooden stand.

Nephrite—6¾ × 4½ × 4 in.
       (17.14 × 11.43 × 10.16 cm.)

Plate 54

Unusually thinly cut libation cup of sea-mist-green jade in the form of a hibiscus blossom supported by stems and foliage. The bats playing on the surface indicate good fortune, as also do the peaches in the foliage. Tibetan-style carving.

The sacred mushroom shape, which is so often seen in the heads of Jui (scepters), is included in the finely carved base. Notice again the use of a very lightweight and delicate base holding up the main body of the carving. The eye is tricked by the seemingly fragile support for so large and heavy a cup. (See Plate 70.)

With carved wooden base.

Nephrite—7¾ in. × 4 in. diameter
(19.68 × 10.16 cm.)

Plate 55

Fantasy in weight and color. This ceremonial pot, adapted from the I Form, is suspended in its frame of pomegranate stems, fruit, and leaves. The color is fine and pure celadon. The boy sitting on the handle forms a holding piece for the lid.
With carved wooden stand.

Nephrite—6½ × 7¼ × 3 in.
(16.51 × 18.41 × 7.62 cm.)

Plate 56

One of a pair of rare, eggshell carved, pale sea mist (almost white) low jade bowls. The flower (stylized chrysanthemum) radiates from the center of the bowl to the beginning of the side rise. The sides are carved in full relief over raised panels both inside and out. The flower is incised onto the bottom of the bowl, and a raised ring foot of the most delicate carving is confined inside.

Note carefully the weight of the pieces with respect to their size. Each piece weighs 2.08 ounces or 65 grams. The very high-gloss finish makes the unbelievable task of carving seem even more difficult. With carved stands.

Jadeite—1 in. × 7½ in. diameter
      (2.54 × 19.05 cm.)

Plates 57, 58, and 59

Three-piece perfumer, including rose-petal bowl, cover, and stand. The jade is mottled moss green in "agate gray." The base, Plate 59, has five half-ball feet connected with a meander pattern band. Five Ming-type legs rest on the band supporting the major side board, which is pierced and carved in blossoms and foliage.

The center of the base is also carved with stylized blossoms and foliage. The bowl is set on a returned lip, which supports sides decorated in poetic interpretations of archaic designs. The handles are most unusual as they show a strong Lamaistic influence in flowers, surrounded and supported by open-carved foliage. The cover, Plate 58, is most intricately cut, being completely pierced wherever possible. Cloud and foliage decorations form an overall pattern topped by an open cut ball serving as finial.

Jadeite—7¾ × 6½ in.
          (19.68 × 16.51 cm.)

Plate 58

Plate 59

Dove-gray jade carved as an urn with loose ring handles in the mouths of dragons. The right side (front view) has a vein of white from which are carved two ptarmigans and a cock pheasant in peonies.

The finial is another bird connected to the body of the base by a free-carved chain (Plate 61) of great rarity and fineness. The length of the chain is 10 inches. The finesse and delicacy of the carving are outstanding, as is the superb polish on the body of the urn.

With wooden stand.

Jadeite—6½ × 4¾ × 1½ in.
       (16.51 × 12.06 × 3.8 cm.)

Plate 61

Plate 62

The horse of the tempest wind; the mane, breath, and billow of fire are brown "skin" jade. The horse and clouds are a mixture of rare blue, lavender, and sea-mist-green.
With wooden stand.

Jadeite—4½ × 5¾ × 3¼ in.
     (11.43 × 14.6 × 8.25 cm.)

Plate 63

Black and gray with touches of lavender, this piece is carved as the three-legged frog of fable. The God of Plenty (money god) is on its back. The Deity holds coins which are threaded through superbly carved strings of surprising delicacy.
With teakwood stand.

Jadeite—6½ × 4 × 2½ in.
      (16.51 ×10.16 × 6.3 cm.)

Plate 64

The Goddess of Music riding on back of a phoenix bird. Pure white jade and finest of eighteenth-century style and execution. The tail of the bird curves gracefully up behind the figure, giving the effect of a halo around the head of the goddess.
Carving on the stand (which is the original) is of unusually fine quality and depicts in minute detail flowers, birds, and scepters.

Nephrite—9½ × 4½ × 3¼ in.
(24.13 × 11.43 × 8.25 cm.)

Plates 65, 66, 67, and 68

Superb emerald-green covered vessel, in archaic style, with tao-teh dragon masque carvings. The handles (Plate 67) are lion heads with scepter tongues and loose rings. The finial (Plate 66) has two playful lions atop the pyramidal cover headed by the flaming Pearl. The finely carved wood base (Plate 68) is of lignum vitae. The symbol on the stand is one of good fortune and long life.

It is somewhat unusual to find the lion included in the decorative appurtenances of such vessels as the one above. The Lion Shih-tze was indigenous to Southwestern China and was adopted by the Chinese as a symbolic figure at an early date. Popular Occidental belief has it, however, that the Lion was not indigenous to China, but that the Lion, as the emblem of Buddha, was first introduced to the Chinese people at the time the Buddhist faith found favor in the minds of the Chinese Emperors, about A.D. 100. The Buddhist teaching is likened to the "roar of the Lion." We also find innumerable references in Chinese literature to the Lion as symbolic of guardianship, protection, wisdom, boldness, bravery, and an eager advancing spirit. Chinese mythological writings associate the Lion with the Deity Ta Yi Tien Tsun or Wen-shu. The naturalistic semblance of the Lion of the Buddhists was transformed by the Taoists into a "chimera," which became the Chinese emblem of "personal protection," while a pair of Lions became the "protectors of the new faith."

It was the pair of Lions that the Chinese thus placed before their palaces and temples as "protective devices" of their Imperialism and religious ideals. Later these figures became tomb guardians and later still the guardians of private dwellings, as protectors of the "family essences," especially against the anger of the "Sun God" and subsequent "fire destruction." By the middle of the Ming Dynasty small statuettes were carved of these chimera to be placed on the family altar as guardians of the "spiritual influences" and "protectors of the faith."

Jadeite—7⅛ × 4⅜ × 8⅛ in.
(18.10 × 11.11 × 20.6 cm.)

Plate 66

Plate 67

Plate 68

Plate 69

This coupe, of clear celadon, is formed in the shape of a lotus blossom entwined with lotus stem and buds. A small mandarin duck (symbol of fidelity) perches on the lip of the coupe.
The Lien Hua or branch of the lotus is attributed to Ho-Hsien Ku, the only woman member of the group of Immortals. This is symbolic of maidenhood, feminine charm, and purity, and so is the emblem of ideal womanhood.
On floral carved wooden base.

Jadeite—$3\frac{1}{2} \times 5\frac{5}{8} \times 2\frac{3}{4}$ in.
$(8.89 \times 14.22 \times 7.0$ cm.$)$

Plate 70

Vase of foremost quality in which the main vessel is a lotus leaf of bright celadon-green-to-white jade containing specklings of iron red. Leaves, pads, and flowers are amazingly thinly carved with returned lips. Two tiny birds fly along the surface, and a heron plucks a bud from the base.
With carved wooden base.

Jadeite—12 × 6¼ × 4⅜ in.
       (30.48 × 15.87 × 11.11 cm.)

Plate 71

Unique piece of jade in form of koro. Body of the burner is translucent ice-green jade (usually called melting snow because of the grass-green color showing in the white snow). Supported by three feet of dragons (five toes of Imperial rank) and Fo Dog faces at the knees. The body is carved with foliage patterns, and dragon heads hold loose rings in their mouths. One side shows Kylin climbing while the opposite side (front) has a most unusual carving of two dragons climbing in clouds and holding the great Pearl between them.

The remarkable color of the true emerald green in the dragons and Pearl marks this as probably having been made as an Imperial court piece. Covering cap has three rings held by clouds and is capped by a bearded Kylin with some of the emerald-green color.

The basic form is eighteenth-century adaptation of the traditional ting shape.

Jadeite—6¾ × 6½ × 5¾ in.
(17.14 × 16.51 × 14.60 cm.)

CHIA CH'ING PERIOD

Plate 72

A bright spinach jade screen with gold incised decoration.
The plaque depicts a series of palace buildings in the mountains (probably the famous Summer Palace that Ch'ien Lung built in the hills northwest of Peking). A servant brings night-blooming plants into the room, while the Emperor leans from the window of his pavilion and contemplates the moon.
This scene is carved from a series of famous paintings from the period of the Sung Dynasty changed to depict the period of Ch'ien Lung or Chia Ch'ing.
The screen is mounted on a lignum vitae frame carved with serpents, flowers, and other Chinese symbols.

Nephrite—10⅞ × 7⅞ × ⅝ in.
(27.62 × 20.00 × 1.6 cm.)

Plate 73

Circular form having front free standing. Panel with apple-green splashes of openwork carving of phoenix birds and peonies. On the body of the vase are peony and leaf carvings in high relief. Phoenix birds and peony carvings form the finial on the cover.

Similar to the Lung: This object is described in the *Shuo Wen* as "a jade vessel used for 'wishing' or praying for rain." During the later Han period (ca. A.D. 50) Taoist priests used a developed Shan-lei form known as a "dragon jar" to obtain the blessing of rain. During the Sung Dynasty the Lung was used to hold the "Water of the Altar" during a modified type of Quong Service when practiced in the temples preceding the Sacrifice to Imperial Ancestors. During the Ming and Ch'ing dynasties we find the Lung Vase used on the Altar to Heaven during the ritual sacrifice offered to the Rain God.

Although this vase was carved in the Ch'ing period, its artistic origins are in the Chou period.

Jadeite—13¼ × 3½ × 5¼ in.
      (33.65 × 8.89 × 13.33 cm.)

Plate 74

This figure of Pindola-Bharadvaja is set in a characteristic pose, holding the Kalasa or Alms Bowl, in a carved shrine. He is one of the Deities known as the "Alms Receiver" included in the Tibetan List of Chen-jen as revised and composed by the Emperor Ch'ien Lung.

This Arhat has been classified as one of the four Disciples of Buddha or Bhikshus, associated with Mahakaayapa, Kundadhana, and Rahula as his compatriots. He and the others were ordered by Buddha, on the latter's death bed, to remain in existence in the Earthly Sphere until the coming of Maitreya.

Pindola-Bharadvaja was first portrayed in the arts about the commencement of the fifth century A.D., when he was associated with his "magical sandalwood bowl."

Su Shih, a celebrated statesman, poet, and commentator who lived A.D. 1036–1101, refers to Pindola-Bharadvaja as the eighteenth Lohan. In A.D. 1756 the Emperor Ch'ien Lung, while visiting Hangchow, altered Su Shih's record of the Lohans and inserted Kasyapa in the place of Pindola-Bharadvaja as the eighteenth member of Kwan-hsiu's compilation.

To appreciate fully the reasons for the alteration in technique in the works of certain artists where the portrayal has changed from a distinctive Buddhist type to one characterizing a Lamaistic influence, it should be remembered that with the advent of the eighteenth century and the reign of Ch'ien Lung, the Emperor, for political reasons, supported in a fervent way certain practices of the "Yellow Sect." Monasteries were erected in various parts of the empire to house the Lamaistic priests, and very quickly the Imperial ritualistic jade cutters were occupied in producing suitable Lamaistic Cult statuettes for use on the temple altars, and for inclusion along with the other altar paraphernalia already located in the private homes of the high officials of state.

In the Ta Fo-Szu Temple in Jehol there existed an excellent set of statuettes representing the Eighteen Lohans, or Disciples of Buddha as they are today generally listed in China. It is in the semblance of such portrayals that the specimen we are now considering found its inspiration.

The bowl held by the Lohan is also of more than passing interest as it too derives its form from the ancient ritualistic forebears which are now believed by some to have originated in the Kalasa of India. This bowl was not a feeding utensil but a type of religious symbol (humility).

The shrine, in which the Lohan sits, is a jagged rockery carving with red "skin" coloration on the side and back. He wears the royal headdress, beads, and robes.

The pieces were made in China but closely followed the Lamaistic styles of India and Tibet.

With molded fitted wooden stand.

Nephrite—10 × 8¾ × 2 in.
(25.40 × 22.22 × 5.08 cm.)

Plate 75

Flower holder of celadon-green jade with inclusions of rust-brown jade. The moon is seen rising through branches of the prunus tree in blossom (classic symbol of spring). Full relief of branches and undercutting from the main body of the stone are excellent. The finish on the moon is very fine.

Again, the sculptor utilized the natural coloration of the jade, producing a clouded effect on the surface of the moon. These inclusions (iron) give the piece a much more subtle air than perhaps it would have without their typifying the almost poetic familiarity of the stone carver with his material.

The shape is based on the archaic I Form and illustrates the freedom with which the eighteenth-century workers used and adapted ancient forms.

Nephrite—8½ × 10 × 2⅞ in.
       (21.59 × 25.40 × 7.30 cm.)

Plate 76

Covered temple urn of unusually fine dark-blue jade tao-teh masques band the center of the vase which otherwise has a perfectly smooth finish. The handles of lotus leaves in scepter form hold free-carved ring handles. The top is surmounted by Fo Dog in playful stance and is banded by shapes of spirit locks.

Students of jade should carefully note the color of the nephrite material. It is most unusual to find a piece so large with so strong and pronounced a blue.

I am informed by Professor Na of the National Palace Museum, Taiwan, that there are some pieces of this quality in their museum; however, they are seldom shown.

Nephrite—12 × 5 × 3 in.
(30.48 × 12.70 × 7.62 cm.)

Plate 77

Figural group of three goats caught in a whirlwind. The color ranges from pale mutton-fat through celadon-green to an intense rust-brown. The carving and polish would indicate a dating from the period of Chia Ch'ing in the early part of the nineteenth century.

The subject is a motif developed during the Ch'ing period and always consists of three sheep or goats with the sun and clouds of wind. The implication of the animals and the sun is good fortune and happiness. With carved wooden stand.

Nephrite—2½ × 6½ × 2½ in.
(6.3 × 16.51 × 6.3 cm.)

Plate 78

Pair of bright spinach jade bowls in eggshell-thin carvings. Finest quality. The handles are hibiscus blossoms and leaves, with vines holding loose ring handles. The rolled edges of the bowls indicate the date. The sides of the bowls are relief carved, inside and out, with hibiscus vines, classical meander pattern, and Kylin heads. The four feet are all undercut in the classical strap-and-buckle designs.
One must consider the extremely difficult job of the carver in handling this type of work, as the slightest pressure would irreparably damage the piece.
With carved wooden stands.

Nephrite—2 × 9 × 6½ in.
        (5.08 × 22.86 × 16.51 cm.)

Plate 79

Pair of hand-cut jadeite chopsticks. Extremely fine and clear bright-green jade graduating from apple to emerald color. The shaping changes from square finger ends to the round end used in the handling of food.

Jadeite—10¼ in. long × ¼ in. square × ³⁄₁₆ in. round
(26.03 × 0.63 × 0.47 cm.)

Plate 80

Set of eight horses. Six jadeite (each a different color, including lavender), one rose quartz, and one carnelian.
Each horse represents one of the various conditions of the wind: quiet pose of the breeze, fury of the tempest, etc.
Each on its own teakwood stand with inlaid silver cloisonné.

Horses are approximately 3 to 5 in. long $\times$ 2 to 3 in. high and 1 in. wide.
(7.62 to 12.7 $\times$ 5.08 to 7.62 $\times$ 2.54 cm.)

Plate 81

Buddha, in gray-white jade, seated in lotus form, with hand in position of supplication. Royal robes and drapery contrast with the humility of the position.
With wooden stand.

Nephrite—6¾ × 4¾ × 1¾ in.
            (17.14 × 12.06 × 4.5 cm.)

Plate 82

Pair of spinach-green jade birds of paradise on sculptured bases. This is the first purchase made for my collection, in 1944.

Nephrite—3¾ × 2 × 9¾ in. high
(9.52 × 5.08 × 24.78 cm.)

Plate 83

Carved in apple-green-and-white jadeite. The Goddess of Music, seated upon the Horse of the Breezes, carries the Koto (stringed instrument).
The Jade Beauty Girl of the Matchmakers is holding the shield of eternity, and The Golden Boy is leading the Horse.
With carved wooden stand.

Jadeite—9¼ × 7¼ × 2 in.
(23.43 × 18.41 × 5.08 cm.)

TAO KUANG PERIOD

Plate 84

Light spinach-green jade with shadings of brown "skin." Two figures: the God of Money with coins on a rope, one coin being carved free; the other figure is the God of Plenty (Buddhist symbol) with one foot on three-toed Frog. From the latter's basket comes the cloud with the Bat of Longevity and the Lotus Flower and Bud of Fertility.
With wooden stand.

Nephrite—10⅞ in. high $\times$ 7½ in. long $\times$ 3¼ in. wide
(27.62 $\times$ 19.05 $\times$ 8.25 cm.)

Plate 85

Pair of extremely fine libation bowls. Dark spinach-green with symbol of two fishes in bottom of bowls. The serpent and monster masque decoration is carved in superb bas-relief on strap handles of Shang style.
With carved fitted wooden stands.

Nephrite—2 in. high × 9¼ in. diameter
(5.08 × 23.43 cm.)

Plate 86

Massive mountain, in light spinach-green jade, carved front and back. This is an especially fine example of Chinese veneration of period style repetition without a negative attitude toward "reproductions." The whole attitude is carved in the style of the Ming period but was done in the Ch'ing period. The polish is typical of the matte finish so usual in Ming pieces. The undercutting and full relief figures indicate its Ch'ing manufacture.

The front shows two ladies holding fans and climbing a meandering path to a mountain retreat. Chinese pines in full and bas-relief alternate with waterfalls among the rocks. On the back, pines and willows grow up to clouds at the top.

It is interesting to the collector, in the classification of period styles and techniques of jade carving, to note the different approach to the foliage carving in this piece to the carving of the eighteenth century as exemplified by the disk screens of Plates 39 and 40.

With fitted wooden stand.

Nephrite—10½ in. high × 7 in. wide × 3 in. long
(26.67 × 17.78 × 7.62 cm.)

Plate 87

True tricolor jade statue of Kuan-Yin. Unusually fine and strong lavender color with contrasting green and rust browns in prunus blossoms. Flowing robes delicately carved. The Goddess is carrying a basket of flowers.

Here is a prime example of the care with which stone and design are coordinated before any work is done. The carver has placed the figure in perfect agreement with the coloring of the stone to achieve that rare quality of perfect naturalness so typical of the Chinese jade carver's art.

With carved wooden stand.

Jadeite—9¾ × 4¼ × 2½ in.
       (24.78 × 10.79 × 6.3 cm.)

ORNAMENTAL USE OF JADE

Peking and most of China are in a zone where the winters are bleak and colorless. During the Ch'ing Dynasty colorful artificial flowers were fashioned. The leaves generally were celadon jade, and the flowers were made of various colored jade, amethyst, coral, carnelian, turquoise. These flowered trees were embedded in handsome cloisonné pots. Within the last fifteen years thousands of these trees were mass-produced in modern China. They are readily recognized, as much of the jade is of a poor quality and some is dyed. The coloring is not permanent and eventually fades. The same holds true of other carvings, such as hard-stone fruit depicting grapes, bananas, and so on. These objects often are not jade but onyx, serpentine, bowenite, aventurine, and lesser hard-stone material. The leaves are generally thick and coarse compared to the refined carvings of the originals. Many are also made of soft soapstone.

Plate 88

Excellent quality of mineral flowers carved of jade, carnelian, amethyst, coral, and rose quartz in a basket made of unusually fine cloisonné.
The flower basket rests on a wooden base.

16 × 14 in.
(40.64 × 35.56 cm.)
Ch'ing Dynasty
Hsien Feng period—A.D. 1851–1861

Plate 89

Mineral flowers and leaves made of jade, turquoise, and carnelian in a basket of fine cloisonné.
On wooden base.

10 × 12 in.
(25.40 × 30.48 cm.)
Ch'ing Dynasty
Probably Hsien Feng period—A.D. 1851–1861

USE OF JADE IN JEWELRY

Today some of the most exquisite and costly jewelry is made of emerald-green Burma jadeite. During the second half of the nineteenth century strings or necklaces of beautiful jadeite beads were assembled. Some were as large as 16 mm. (⅝ in.) in diameter. Uniform bead sizes were favored before 1900, but since then the easier graduated sizes have been made. However, very few necklaces are in existence today. Most have been disassembled and the individual beads cut in two, making cabochons or caps for rings and other decorative objects.

Plate 90

Two strings of bright apple-green jade beads:
1. Containing 35 beads approximately 15 mm. diameter.
2. Containing 36 beads approximately 16 mm. diameter.

Both strings are of unusual high translucency and uniformity of color. This type of string has not been produced since the turn of the twentieth century. Beads produced since then have usually been of the graduated type.

Jadeite of jewelry quality carved probably during the middle of the nineteenth century.

Despite the fact that the finest color photography available was used, only the human eye can appreciate the subtlety of shading in this fascinating stone. Light seems to emanate from the center of the stone itself rather than diffuse light from a source outside.

Plate 91

This amulet is of highly translucent jadeite carved during the early nineteenth century. Material and carving are superb and often referred to as "Imperial Quality."
The front shows a phoenix bird surrounded by the Sacred Fungus of Immortality. Bamboo and cherry blossoms are portrayed on both sides.

1½ in. wide × 2½ in. long × ⅛ in. thick
(3.8 × 6.3 × 0.3 cm.)

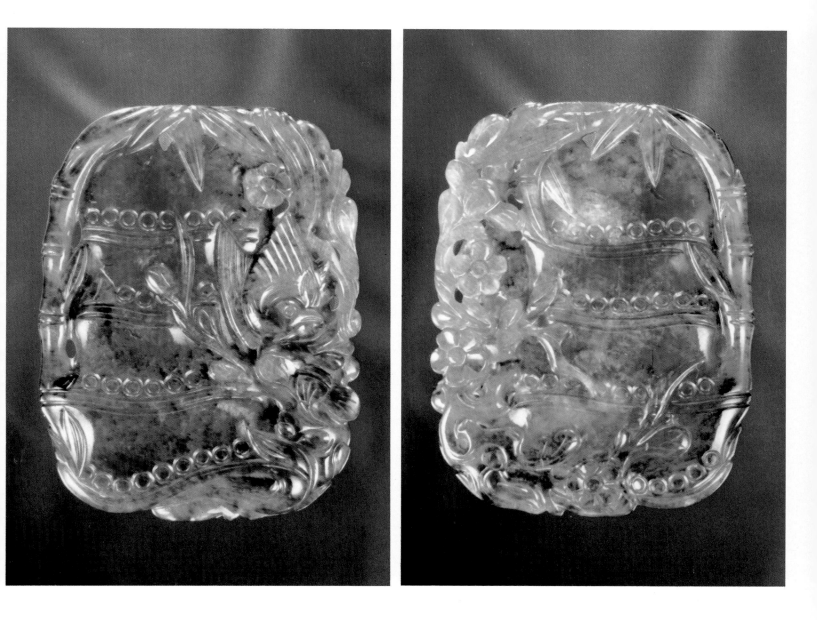

OIL EWERS

Plate 92

Two oil ewers, probably from an altar. The first piece is of the Ch'ien Lung period, carved in ice-green jade, almost white (nephrite). The ancient bronze form, decoration, and stylization are repeated in the stone in true imitation of period I Style. The vessel stands on a foot with meander and tablet decoration. The spout extends from the mouth of a mythical bird whose body forms the main tank of the ewer. A loose ring hangs from the breast of the bird, and stylized tail feathers from the handle. The top is carefully cut to the form of the base surmounted by a phoenix bird.

Legend says that a jade carver of the middle nineteenth century boasted of carving equally well as any artist during the Ch'ien Lung period; thus, he produced a duplicate of the white nephrite ewer in green jadeite. However, upon close examination, I found the work of the Ch'ien Lung artist superior.

With wooden bases.

5⅞ × 4¾ × 1⅛ in.
(14.92 × 12.06 × 2.9 cm.)

MONGOLIAN OBJECTS

Early in the nineteenth century ornamental silver castings of koros, wine containers, and similar objects appeared in Mongolia. Many old jade articles, such as girdle clasps, pieces of mandarin collars, Pi's, were incorporated, along with inlays of coral, malachite, amethyst, and other semiprecious stones.

Plate 93

Silver wine pot with mounts of coral, turquoise, and jade. Jade plaques, from the Ming Dynasty, T'ai Ch'ang period, A.D. 1620, contain goose and lotus designs for a happy and fruitful marriage.
With wooden stand.

10½ × 8¾ × 3¼ in.
(26.67 × 22.22 × 8.25 cm.)

Plate 94

Antique silver basket set with coral, malachite, and carved white jade. Jade produced during Ming Dynasty, Wan Li period—A.D. 1573–1619.

12 × 7½ × 7½ in.
(30.48 × 19.05 × 19.05 cm.)

Plate 95

Pair of incised silver vases in the T'ang Style, ca. 1830. Designs of dragon masques and mounts with turquoise and coral jewels. Contains four Pi's of early Ming jade (2½ in. diameter). Pi is the symbol of Heaven and the beneficent dragon brings spring rain.
With wooden stands.

10 × 4½ × 3½ in.
(25.40 × 11.43 × 8.89 cm.)
Lung Ch'ing period—A.D. 1567–1572

Plate 96

Covered urn (koro) of Mongolian silver tracery encrusted with insets of malachite, turquoise, coral, and jade. Early garment closures are mounted on sides and top. Jade carving of Ming origin.

8¼ in. × 5¼ in. diameter
(20.96 × 13.33 cm.)

Plate 97

Open rectangular Mongolian silver urn with jade garment closures as feet (Ming period) and four panels of three-layer carved white jade dragons.

7⅝ × 7⅜ × 4⁵⁄₁₆ in.
(19.37 × 18.73 × 10.94 cm.)
Ch'ing Dynasty
Tao Kuang period—A.D. 1821–1850

BIBLIOGRAPHY

I possess a small library of books on the subject of jade and, from knowledge gathered, prepared the text, thus enabling the novice collector to follow a few guidelines before entering the bottomless pool of the art of jade.

Goette, John, *Jade Lore*, 1937.

Gump, Richard, *Jade Stone of Heaven*, 1962.

Hansford, S. Howard, *Chinese Carved Jades*, 1968.

——, *Essence of Hills and Stream*, 1969.

Hartman, Joan M., *Chinese Jade of Five Centuries*.

Lefebure d'Argence, René, *Avery Brundage Collection, Chinese Jades*, 1972.

Luzzatto-Bilitz, Oscar, *Antique Jade*, 1969.

Nott, Stanley Charles, *Chinese Jade in the Stanley Charles Nott Collection*. Norton Gallery and School of Art, West Palm Beach, Florida, 1942.

Pope-Hennessy, Una, *Early Chinese Jade*, 1923.

Whitlock, Herbert P., and Ehrman, Martin L., *The Story of Jade* 1965.

Wills, Geoffrey, *Jade of the East*, 1973.